Rosario + Vampire

Season II

2

AKIHISA IKEDA

Horror Story Thus Far
Tsukune Aono accidentally enrolls in Yokai Academy, a high school for monsters! After befriending the school's cutest girl, Moka Akashiya, he decides to stay...even though Yokai has a zero-tolerance policy toward humans. (A *fatal* policy.) Tsukune has to hide his true identity while fending off attacks by monster gangs. He survives with the help of his News Club friends—Moka, Kurumu, Yukari and Mizore.
But then a student riot nearly destroys the school, and classes are canceled for half a year for "remodeling." It's already spring by the time the gang (now sophomores) return... and meet Moka's rowdy little sister, Koko, who has enrolled as a freshman. When a phantom attacker terrorizes the school, Moka and Koko rush into the campus's underground dungeons to apprehend the culprit—but end up being the next victims. The rest of the News Club is in hot pursuit. But will they be in time to save their friends...?
Tsukune Aono
Only his close friends know he's the lone human at Yokai and the only one who can pull off Moka's rosario. Due to repeated infusions of Moka's blood, he sometimes turns into a ghoul.
Moka Akashiya
The school beauty, adored by every boy. Transforms into a powerful vampire when the "rosario" around her neck is removed. Favorite food: Tsukune's blood! ♡

Kurumu Kurono

A succubus. Also adored by all the boys—for two obvious reasons. Fights with Moka over Tsukune.

Yukari Sendo

A mischievous witch. Much younger than the others. A genius who skipped several grades.

Mizore Shirayuki

A snow fairy who manipulates ice. She fell in love with Tsukune after reading his newspaper articles. ♡

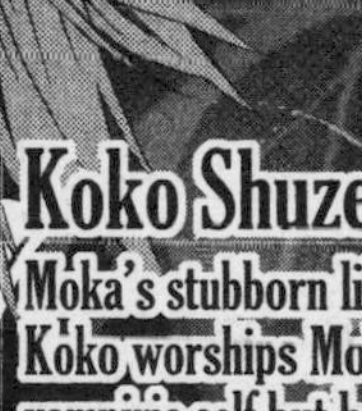

Koko Shuzen

Moka's stubborn little sister. Koko worships Moka's inner vampiric self but hates her sweet exterior. Koko's pet bat transforms into a weapon.

Ruby Tojo

Proud disciple of the late witch Lady Okata. Only learned to trust humans after meeting Tsukune. Now assist Yokai's headmaster.

Shizuka Nekonome

Tsukune and friends' homeroom teacher and News Club advisor. Loves fish. ♡

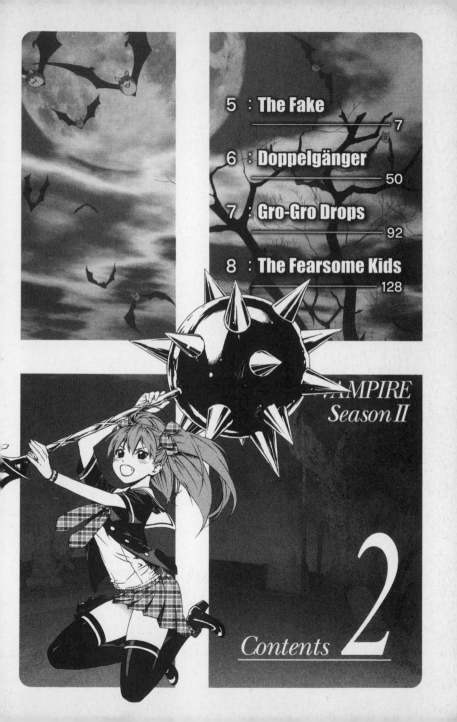

VAMPIRE
Season II

Contents 2

5: The Fake

ROSARIO+VAMPIRE

Season II

HNGH...? WH... WHERE AM I?
HOW'D I GET HERE?

THAT'S WEIRD... I HURT ALL OVER...
WHAT'S GOING ON...?

AWAKE ...?
YOU'RE ACTUALLY PRETTY TOUGH.
!
I THOUGHT YOUR BONES WERE CRUSHED TO DUST.
WHA ...?

UNFOR-TUNATELY FOR YOU, YOU WOKE UP...
...JUST IN TIME FOR ME TO KILL YOU.

WH-WHO ARE YOU?!

NNH ...

M...MOKA?!

NOT JUST MOKA...
OTHER STUDENTS TOO...

NOW I REMEMBER! THE PHANTOM ATTACKER!
HEADS UP!!
WE'VE GOT A STORY!!
WE CAME HERE TO FIND WHOEVER WAS ATTACKING YOKAI STUDENTS...
A PHANTOM ATTACKER!
STILL

...AND WE GOT JUMPED!
SO...
...YOU'RE THE PHANTOM ATTACKER?!

"PHANTOM ATTACKER"?
FIRST OF ALL, THAT'S A REALLY LAME NAME. SECOND... NO, I'M NOT.

KLIK
WE'RE A BAND OF THIEVES. SERIOUS THIEVES.
CHECK OUT OUR HAUL!

THIS TIME WE KNOCKED OVER AN ARMORED CAR. ♡

FSSHHHH

RRRK

THE MONEY IS... DRENCHED IN BLOOD! WHAT DID THEY DO?!

THESE GUYS WOULD KILL US WITHOUT A SECOND THOUGHT!
GWWH
WE'VE GOT TO GET OUT OF HERE!
I HAVE TO RESCUE MOKA—AND FAST!
HOOOOO

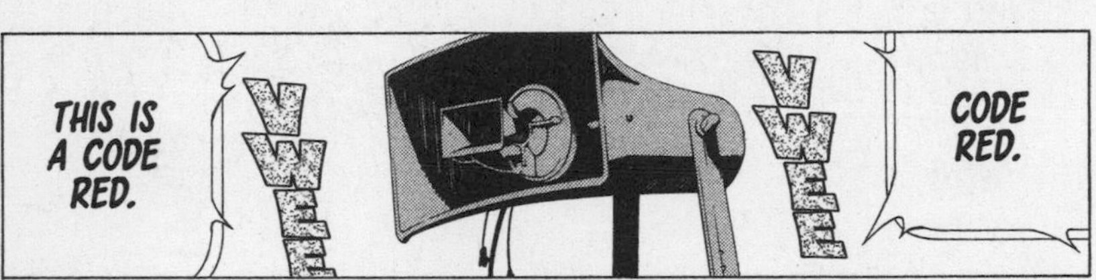
CODE RED.
VWEE
THIS IS A CODE RED.
VWEE

A GROUP OF THIEVES HAVE INVADED THE SCHOOL GROUNDS.
SEVERAL STUDENTS HAVE BEEN WOUNDED, AND THE PERPETRATORS ARE HIDING ON CAMPUS.
VWEE
FOR YOUR SAFETY, RETURN TO YOUR CLASSROOMS AND LOCK THE DOORS.
VWEE

I REPEAT...
RABBL
RABBL
RABBL
...
GEEZ.
WHAT A DRAG.

MOVE IT, SQUIRT.
YOU'RE GOIN' THE WRONG WAY.
BWMP
AH!

THIS IS REALLY, REALLY, REALLY BAD!

AAGH

WE WERE LOOKING FOR ONE PHANTOM— AND WE FOUND A WHOLE GANG!
AND TSUKUNE AND MOKA RUSHED IN WITHOUT A CLUE!
RABBL RABBL
TOTAL WORST-CASE SCENARIO!

I CAN'T STAND IT! I CAN'T, I CAN'T!
YAAA!
FLAIL FLAIL
UM... YUKARI?
!

WHAT ARE YOU DOING?
UH...

RUBY!

ACK!

BING!

Witch
Ruby Tojo

SORRY I HAVEN'T COME TO VISIT MUCH.

EVEN NOW, I'M ACTUALLY ON PATROL FOR—

WHAT DO WE DO NOW?

?

AND PART OF MY JOB DESCRIPTION IS TO...
...ENSURE THE SAFETY OF THE STUDENT BODY!
ZM
WHAT THE HELL ARE YOU TALKING ABOUT?!!
Eek!
TSUKUNE HASN'T...
YES?
GASP
I MEAN, HE ISN'T...
NOTHING, NOTHING. JUST TELL ME WHAT'S GOING ON.
YOU'LL HELP?!
OF COURSE I'LL HELP! TSUKUNE SAVED MY LIFE.

...IF WE'RE GOING TO SAVE TSUKUNE AND MOKA!

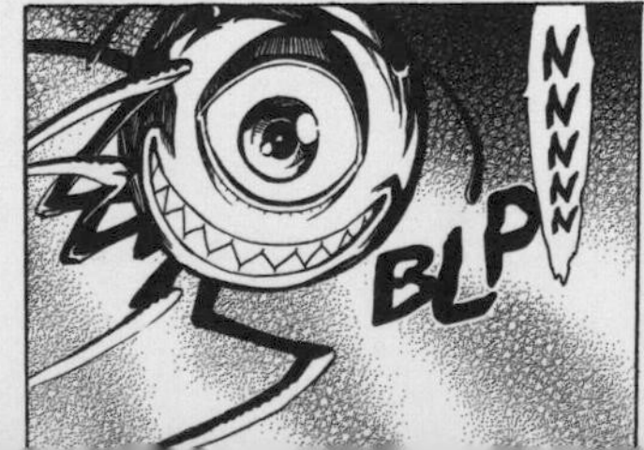

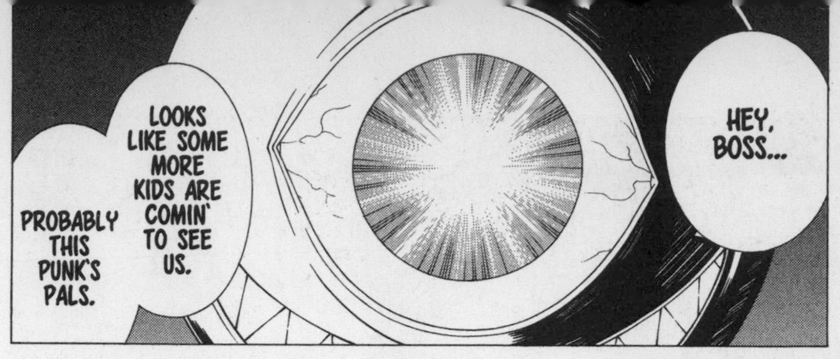

HEY, BOSS...
LOOKS LIKE SOME MORE KIDS ARE COMIN' TO SEE US.
PROBABLY THIS PUNK'S PALS.

...

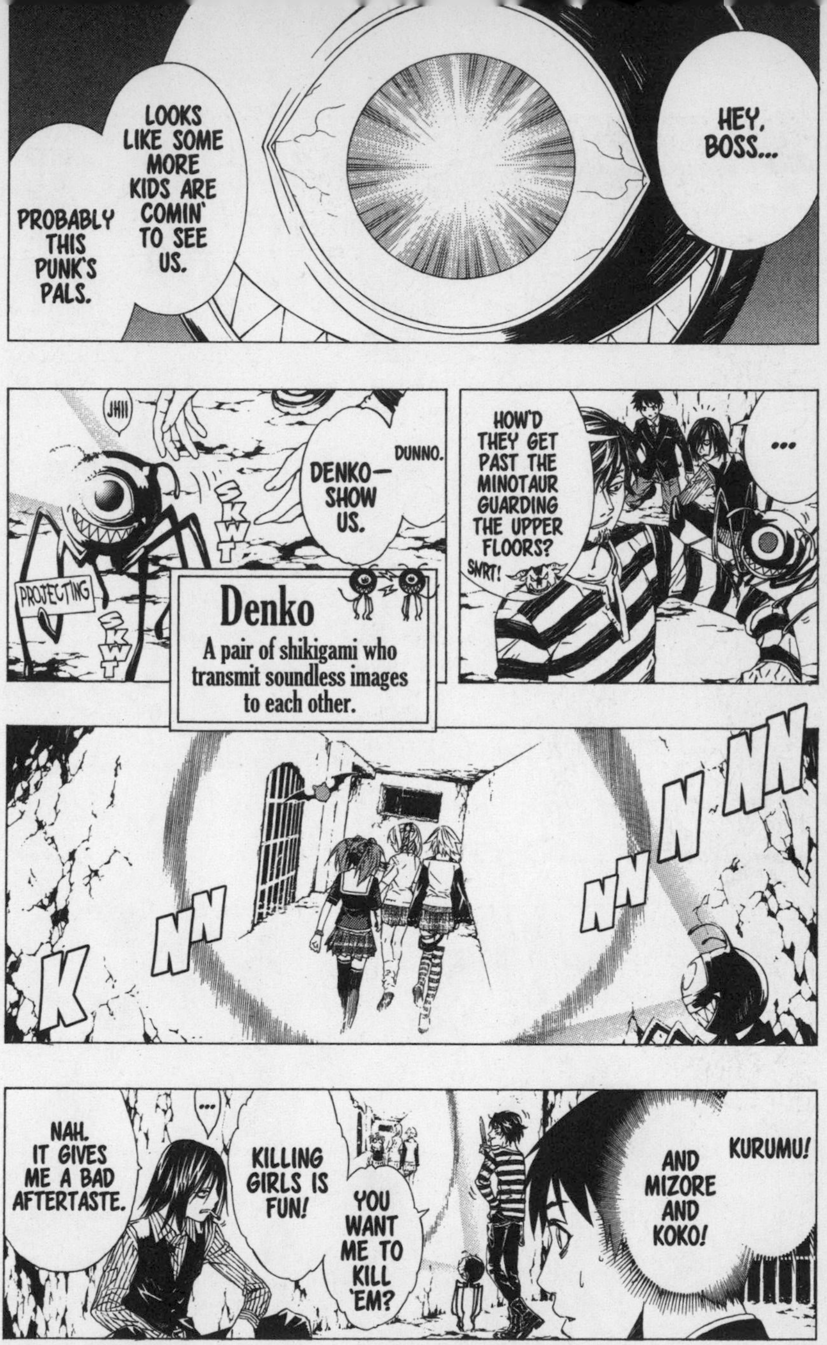

HOW'D THEY GET PAST THE MINOTAUR GUARDING THE UPPER FLOORS?

SNRT!

DUNNO.

DENKO— SHOW US.

JHII

SKWT

SKWT

PROJECTING

Denko
A pair of shikigami who transmit soundless images to each other.

K NN NN N NN

KURUMU!
AND MIZORE AND KOKO!
YOU WANT ME TO KILL 'EM?
KILLING GIRLS IS FUN!
...
NAH. IT GIVES ME A BAD AFTERTASTE.

YOU GOTTA GET OVER THAT.
I MEAN, COME ON! AFRAID OF GIRLS?
YOU HAVEN'T EVEN *TOUCHED* THAT FINE ONE OVER THERE.

I'M NOT *AFRAID* OF GIRLS! THEY JUST DON'T DO ANYTHING FOR ME.
TCH
I COULD KILL 'EM ANYTIME I WANT TO...
PWF
SHW
RRK

W-WHAT ...?
...WITH MY POWERS.

ZAKKK

COOL, HUH? LIKE LOOKING IN A MIRROR.
...
SSSS
SSS
I ABSORB FACES THROUGH MY LEFT HAND...AND TRANSFER THEM WITH MY RIGHT.
THINK OF IT AS A KIND OF... COPY-AND-PASTE TECHNIQUE.
COPY → PASTE
A
A
B

WHENEVER WE GOTTA MAKE A QUICK GETAWAY...
I JUST KIDNAP SOMEONE AND PASTE THEIR FACE ONTO ALL MY GUYS.
THAT'S WHY NOBODY HAS THE FOGGIEST WHAT WE LOOK LIKE!
!!

MY LI'L TRICK ALSO COMES IN HANDY FOR *MURDER.*

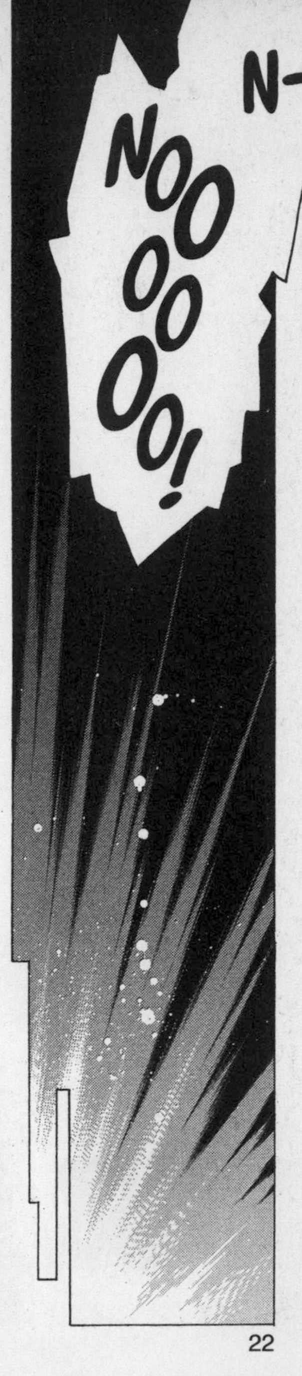
N-NOOOOOOO!

...

ISN'T THIS KIND OF WEIRD?
WE'VE BEEN WALKING FOR A LONG TIME...
...BUT WE'RE NOT GETTING ANY CLOSER.

COME TO...
...THINK OF IT... IT FEELS LIKE WE'VE BEEN GOING IN CIRCLES!
SO...

YAAAA
I'M TAKING THE LEAD—LIKE I SHOULD HAVE FROM THE START!
OH NO, YOU DON'T! *I'M* GONNA FIND TSUKUNE AND RESCUE HIM!
YOU COULDN'T FIND YOUR OWN...

OW!
OW OW!
TMP
HUH ...?
YOU GUYS CAME ALL THIS WAY TO FIND *ME*?
!!
UH...
THANKS, BUT...
WE GOT THE PHANTOM ALREADY. IT'S OVER.
MMMMD

NO!

DON'T BE FOOLED!

...SEE HIM FOR WHAT HE IS!
TSUKUNE!

I'M SO GLAD YOU'RE SAFE!
HEH HEH... I'M FINE!

PIECE OF CAKE...
NONE OF THEM SUSPECTS A THING.
GRR

SOMETIMES, MY POWERS EVEN SCARE ME!
COME CLOSER, SWEETHEART... SO I CAN KILL YOU.

THAT'S GOOD. CLOSER...
CLOSER...

AGH...

OOSH

TOO CLOSE!

G

WHAT'D I TELL YOU?

...

THE BOSS CAN'T HANDLE WOMEN.
HE TURNS RED AS A TOMATO IF THEY JUST LOOK HIM IN THE EYE. AND...
HHHHHHHHHHHH
IT LOOKS LIKE HE PASSES OUT WHEN THEY...
I'LL NEVER COMPLAIN ABOUT KURUMU'S SMOTHERING HUGS AGAIN!

WHAT THE...?
NO! CAN'T LET THEM GET TO ME...

MY MISSION IS TO KILL THESE GIRLS.
BOOBS ARE... HARMLESS! HARMLESS, YOU HEAR?!

THERE THEY ARE!
ARE YOU OKAY?!
!

HEY, YUKARI!

AND RUBY! COOL!

MORE OF THEM! AND EVERY ONE— FEMALE!

SHUK

...KUUU...
OKAY ...
ONE DOWN ...
?!
TSU-KUNE! I'M SHOCKED!
I NEVER THOUGHT YOU'D BE SO... ROUGH!
UH...

PLEASE...
...DON'T STOP!
GAK!
WHO ARE THESE KIDS?
WHAT ARE THEY TRYIN' TO DO TO ME?!
OHHHH
PANT PANT
SCARY... SO SCARY...
WELL, IF WE'RE GOING TO TROT OUT OUR PERSONAL FETISHES...
Mm...
...THIS IS WHAT I LIKE! HOW 'BOUT YOU, TSUKUNE?!
NYA HA HA HA HA
EVEN THE LITTLE GIRL?!
THIS TSUKUNE GUY MUST BE SOME KINDA PERVERT!
GWH
GK
FWP
FWP

SORRY, YUKARI... I GUESS YOU LEAVE HIM COLD.

PLINK

ICE!

PLINK

CAN'T BELIEVE HE JUST WALKED UP TO ME AND...
HFF HFF
!

HUH...?
SNF SNF SNF
WHAT?
!

SHLP

WHAT ARE YOU DOING?!
GROSS!
YOU TASTE LIKE CIGA-RETTES!
PWH PWH PWH
?!

WHAT HAVE YOU DONE?! YOU TASTE NASTY ALLUVA SUDDEN!
YOUR ONLY REDEEMING QUALITY WAS THE FLAVOR OF YOUR BLOOD!

??
HUH ?!
WHA...?

OH, COME ON...
AHA HA HA
WHO CARES WHAT MY BLOOD TASTES LIKE?!

GET AWAY FROM HIM!
ZIP
?!

TSUKUNE... WHERE'S YOUR CHAIN?
BDMP BDMP
THE ONE THAT'S ALWAYS WRAPPED AROUND YOUR RIGHT ARM...
...

...AND FASTENED WITH THE *SPIRIT LOCK.*
YOU TOLD US YOU HAVE TO WEAR IT *ALL THE TIME* TO STOP THE VAMPIRE BLOOD INSIDE YOU FROM DEVOURING YOUR BODY...
...AND THAT IF YOU EVER TAKE IT OFF, YOU'LL TURN INTO A *GHOUL.*

TSUKUNE *WITHOUT* THAT SPIRIT LOCK...
...WOULDN'T BE TSUKUNE ANYMORE!

*TO SAVE MORTALLY WOUNDED TSUKUNE, MOKA INJECTED HIM WITH HER VAMPIRIC BLOOD (SEASON I, VOL. 3). THAT BLOOD HAS BEEN BATTLING HIS BODY EVER SINCE.

HOOOOOOOO OOOO

AND WHY WOULD TSUKUNE WONDER...
...WHY SOMEONE WOULD CARE ABOUT THE FLAVOR OF HIS BLOOD... WHEN *THAT*'S WHAT DREW MOKA TO HIM?
WHICH LEAVES ME WITH ONE LAST QUES- TION...
WHO ARE YOU?!

...
HSSS...

DON'T UNDER-ESTIMATE US!

VZZZZ

AAAAAAA

WHSHHH
OH NO, YOU DON'T!!
KRMMMM
GHA
TMMMMMM
MO...
...KA...?
MOKA!

H-HOW LONG HAVE YOU BEEN...
OH, I WOKE UP A WHILE AGO. I WAS JUST...
...WAITING FOR THE RIGHT MOMENT.
SKSHT SKSHT
BUT NOW— WE'VE GOT TO ACT FAST!
TEAR OFF MY ROSARIO!
O... OKAY...
HERE GOES...
THUK

MWK
KRK
YOU WERE DOOMED THE SECOND YOU GOT HERE.
MWK MWK
DON'T GET COCKY.
NWHHHH
THAT'S ONE DOWN...
VWWN
N...

URK...
SPSSHHH
NOOO!
HA HAHA HAHA HA HA HA

W-WHERE'S TSUKUNE?
AND HOW DID YOU...GET HIS FACE?
...
SWH
IS...IS HE...?

SHH...
YEP.
STONE DEAD.
PROBABLY.
!!

ONE OF MY GUYS IS KEEPING AN EYE ON HIM, BUT...
...HE'S A TOTAL PSYCHO.
HA HA
HA HA

AIN'T NOTHIN' HE LIKES BETTER THAN CUTTING PEOPLE INTO LITTLE PIECES.
HE'S A KILLING ARTIST.

AND HE'S HAD TSUKUNE FOR A WHILE, SO... WELL...
I WON'T BORE YOU WITH THE DETAILS.
It's gross.
!!

YOU... MONSTER!!

KRAAAAA

KURUMU, STOP!

VWSH

FIRST WE'VE GOT TO FIND OUT WHERE...

SLISSSH

!!

SPSSH

GO AHEAD AND ATTACK ME, GIRLIE. I'VE GOT NO QUALMS ABOUT HITTING BACK.

YOU BETTER BE READY.

I'M POWERFUL.

AND YOU'RE NEXT!

KA KA KA KA KA KA

HHHHH

Ground Spider

ZZZ W SS

GRRRP
...
JEALOUS? I HAVE *SIX ARMS.*
KNOW WHY I'VE GOT SO MANY?
RRNG
YRNK
SO I CAN HOLD MY PREY DOWN WITH *FOUR* OF 'EM...
WHHH
...AND CUT IT UP WITH THE OTHER TWO.
ALLOW ME TO DEMON-STRATE...
WOOOOOOM
NOOO!

WHERE SHOULD I START?
HERE?
NH...
OR...
SSS
HERE?
HERE?

NO WAY...
TMP

TSUKUNE!
HM...?

YOU WANNA DIE TWICE?!
RAA

I MORTALLY WOUNDED HIM!
NOBODY GETS BACK ON HIS FEET AFTER I...

LET GO...
...OF MOKA.

SCHN
TSUKU...
...UUU...
...NE
!!
SCHN
HAPPY NOW?
HEH HEH
SPURT
HUH?

NOW... WHERE WERE WE? ♡

SPSSSSH

NO! TSUKUNE!

TSUKUNE!

SHUT UP!

GRRP

AH!

WHAT KEEPS YOU GOING...? YOU REALIZE YOU'RE DOOM—

!!
HHH

PLUP

HUH ...?
HEY! THAT... HURT...
GKSH
MY HANDS! C-CRUSHED ...
SPLRT

TMP
GASP

W... WAIT...
HOW DID YOU DO...
...THAT?
HOLD IT! STOP!
I'M SORRY...
CAN'T WE TALK THIS—

TOOOO
OOOOM

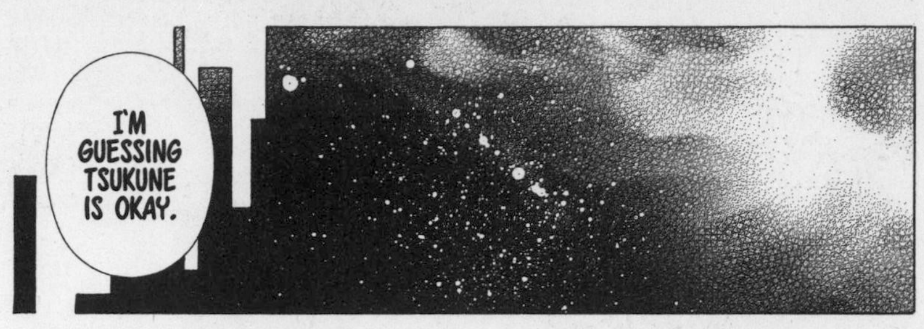
I'M GUESSING TSUKUNE IS OKAY.

RUBY?!
THE VAMPIRE BLOOD MOKA INJECTED INTO TSUKUNE IS DORMANT INSIDE HIS BODY UNTIL...
...TSUKUNE IS IN IMMINENT DANGER. THEN THAT BLOOD GIVES HIM... STRENGTH.

YOU MEAN...
UNFOR-TUNATELY...

FOR THE LAST SIX MONTHS, TSUKUNE'S BEEN LIVING PEACEFULLY IN THE HUMAN WORLD.
KRK

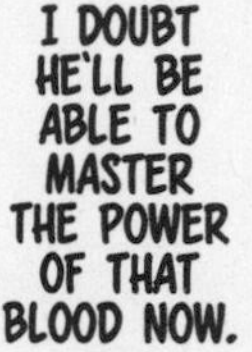
I DOUBT HE'LL BE ABLE TO MASTER THE POWER OF THAT BLOOD NOW.

THIS TIME, HIS BODY COULD BE OVERWHELMED BY...THE FORCE OF THE VAMPIRE.
KRK
PWK

HE MIGHT FINALLY LOSE...HIS HUMANITY.

RRK
RRK

TSU... ...
TSUKU... NE...

6: Doppelgänger

TSUKUNE ...? WHERE ARE YOU GOING ...?
JLSH
DON'T YOU RECOGNIZE ME?

TSUKUNE!
KRMBL
KRMBL
DBMMMMMM

GLNK
GLNK

TMP
IT'S HOPELESS. MY VAMPIRE BLOOD HAS TAKEN HIM OVER.
IF THIS KEEPS UP...
TSUKUNE...

PLEASE...
COME BACK!

...
WHERE ARE THEY?!
WELL?!

TMM TMM TMM TMM TMM

KARATE, KUNG FU, BOXING...

I'VE MASTERED THEM ALL.

SO IF YOU GIRLS ARE THINKING OF TAKING ME ON—

JUST TELL ME WHERE TSUKUNE IS, OR I'LL—
STUFF IT!
WSSH
THP

ZZZH

YOU'RE FAST.
AND I BET YOU'RE WAY STRONGER THAN ME TOO.
?!!
VWM
HOW'D HE DO THAT...?
LUCKY FOR ME...
PWFT
...I'VE GOT ANOTHER, EVEN BETTER WEAPON.
!

FSSS
!!!
FAAA
AA
WH-WHAT ...?
MY PEOPLE'S GIFT IS TO TRANSFORM.
WE CAN BECOME ANYONE.
WSH
POOM
NOT JUST BY ADOPTING THE FACE...
I CAN DUPLI-CATE... EVERY-THING.
BUP
EVEN YOUR STRENGTH AND SPECIAL POWERS.
ZZZHHH
FWAPA

I'M A DOPPELGÄNGER.

WE'RE THIEVES WHO SURVIVE BY STEALING THE LIVES OF OTHERS.

Bite-Size Encyclopedia

Doppelgänger

Literally "double walker" in German. According to legend, those who look upon their doppelgänger are destined to die within a few days. This monster's true appearance is a mystery.

H-HE COPIED HER...
...RIGHT DOWN TO HER... HER...
OH...
!!
...WINGS. TO MY WINGS.

DIDN'T REALIZE YOU WERE HIDING THESE IN YOUR HUMAN FORM...
FWP
FWP
...
MY POWER ISN'T JUST TO SIMULATE AN APPEARANCE... IT'S TO CAPTURE A TRUE FORM.

I FEEL SORT OF OFF BALANCE SOMEHOW THOUGH...
BWM
WHAT THE ...?
BWM
BWM

BWNG
...
BWNG

AGH! IT'S BECAUSE OF THESE THINGS!!
TH-THEY'RE SO...HUGE!!
RRRKKG
SPURT
WATCH WHAT YOU SAY ABOUT MY BODY!!

I'VE NEVER BEEN A GIRL BEFORE ...
AND QUIT SQUEEZING MY BREASTS!!
HFF
HFF HFF
GMG GMG

NOW GET OUT OF MY BODY...
...BEFORE I TEAR MYSELF APART!!
HEY, MAYBE THIS FORM WILL HELP ME GET OVER MY GIRL PHOBIA...
VWMM
NO, IT WON'T!!
MIGHT BE FUN TO LIVE YOUR LIFE FOR A WHILE.
HWSH
HWSH
AFTER ALL, YOU WON'T BE LIVING IT MUCH LONGER. THERE'S JUST NO ROOM...
...
WOOSH
NONE OF MY ATTACKS ARE LANDING...
...FOR YOU AND ME BOTH.
...
MOVE IT, KURUMU!
SH

PKW

M... MIZORE ...?!

K K

SETTLE DOWN! HE'S TOTALLY FLUSTERED YOU!
REMEMBER ALL OUR TRAINING?
Y- YOU'RE RIGHT.
HOOOOOOO

TINK

HM...
POWER OVER ICE...

MIGHT BE FUN TO...
...TAKE YOUR LIFE TOO!
NNNN

AGAINST THE TWO OF US...

...YOU DON'T HAVE A CHANCE!

I *TOLD* YOU...I'VE MASTERED *EVERY* MARTIAL ART.
I CAN DO THINGS WITH THIS BODY THAT YOU COULDN'T *DREAM* OF!

HOOOOO
OOOOOO

...

HE IS BETTER THAN THE TWO OF US...

HE DODGED BOTH OUR ATTACKS—AND COUNTER-ATTACKED!

ZZZ
ZOOP♪
GETTING THE IDEA...?
EVEN ALL TOGETHER YOU DON'T HAVE A CHANCE.

TMM
YOU HAVEN'T FOUGHT ME YE—
TP

WUK

NOW... DIE.
VSSH

CHK

!!!!

VOOOO
TSK, TSK.

WELL, LOOK WHO'S HERE...
CAN'T BELIEVE YOUR HEART'S STILL BEATING ...

TOOM
TSUKUNE!
I'M SO GLAD YOU'RE ALL RIGHT!
TSUKUNE ...?
N...NO WAY. THAT'S A... VAMPIRE AURA.
SO IT'S TRUE...?
MY SISTER REALLY DID INJECT VAMPIRE BLOOD INTO TSUKUNE'S BODY?!

HOOOOOOOOOOOOOOOO

YOU'RE GOOD.

TO GET HERE...

...YOU HAD TO KILL THE GUY I LEFT GUARDING YOU, RIGHT?

WHOA...
FAST THOUGH...
KRMBL
RR...
RRRAGH!
BUT SLOPPY. CLASSIC AMATEUR.

I'LL HIT HIM UNDERHAND...
...FOLLOW UP WITH A COUNTER-PUNCH, THEN STAB HIM IN THE CHEST WITH MY KNIFE HAND.

!!
N...NO! THIS IS BAD...
RUBY?

PERFECT POSITION...

NOW TO FAKE LEFT...

...AND...

...RIGHT AND...

WHK
H
KKKKK
K OOOOOOM

TSUKUNE...?
I WAS AFRAID OF THIS! THE VAMPIRE BLOOD IS TOO STRONG.
TSUKUNE IS BEING... ABSORBED!
SSS
SSS
SSSS

SS SS SS
B-BUT...

NH...
GLNK

S-SO HE'S POWER-FUL...
BLEW THROUGH MY DEFENSES...
COULD HAVE DODGED THAT EASY IF I'D...
YOU...

VWHH

WAIT, WAIT!

CAN'T WE...

...TALK THIS THROUGH?

ZHHHH

HAHA...

HA HA HA HA...

AHA HAHA HAHA HAHA...

WHWH

ZH

HE'S GONE ON A RAMPAGE— A GHOULISH RAMPAGE!
HE MIGHT NOT EVEN BE HUMAN ANYMORE!
DGMMM
WAAGH!
HELP ME, YUKARI!
WE'VE GOT TO STOP TSUKUNE! BUT HOW—?!
VWH

THINK!
GOTTA FOCUS!
HSS
THERE MUST BE A WAY TO STOP HIM.
HE'S GOT TO HAVE A WEAKNESS...

RAAAA
A WEAK-NESS!
OH!
NO! THAT CREEP IS GOING TO—

HOLD IT RIGHT THERE!

RRRRRIP

AAAGH!

SPURT

DOOOOOOOOOM

THANK GOD!! HE'S STILL *HUMAN!!*

OF COURSE! THE UNIVERSAL MALE WEAKNESS!

VWHH

HA HA HA HA HA HA

YEEEEEEE

PUT MY CLOTHES BACK ON THIS INSTANT!!

DEMON WALL

TSUKUNE ...

HEH

AND WHERE DO YOU THINK YOU'RE GOING ...?

TMP

YOU STILL HAVE TO GIVE ME BACK MY SISTER!

RGH... ONE AFTER ANOTHER...
VWSH
TIME TO RUN? DITCH THE OTHERS AND THE LOOT AND...DIS-APPEAR?
TM
TM
STOP!
YOU WON'T GET AWAY FROM ME!
TM
TM
...
!
JLSH
TM
TM
TM
TM
THD
UNH!
?!!
DAMN...
THD
WHAT NOW...?
!
OH...
I SAID... STOP!!
TA

!!

KBMMMMMMMM

WHAT ...?
GLNK
HA HA...

HAHAHA! I GOT LUCKY!
GLNK
OOOO
PERFECT TIMING. JUST THE GIRL I WANTED TO BUMP INTO!

I SENSED SOMETHING ABOUT HER...
TA
SOME-THING SPECIAL...
Nnh...
SOME-THING I WANTED TO... BECOME.

AND...
...MY INSTINCTS WERE RIGHT!
TA
TA
ZWP
ZWPP

TH-THAT AWFUL AURA...
DON'T TELL ME...
TATATATATA

BENEATH THAT SWEET SURFACE... WHAT POWER!!
MOKA...!
HE'S TURNED INTO THE INNER MOKA—THE VAMPIRIC VERSION!

NOT GOOD. NOT AT ALL.
IF HE GOT THAT POWERFUL TURNING INTO *YOU*, KURUMU...
WHAT'LL HE BE LIKE AS *HER?!*

HM... SO THAT CROSS ...
...WAS SOME KIND OF SEAL...
...THAT SUPPRESSED THIS *MAGNIFICENT* POWER.
CHLNK

WHAT A PATHETIC WASTE... ALL THAT POWER...
...WASTED ON A TIMID LITTLE FOOL AFRAID TO LET IT LOOSE AND PLAY WITH IT.

KRK
WELL...
YOU CAN ALL DIE NOW.

HWF
YOU BIG PHONY!
YOU'LL NEVER TAKE MY SISTER'S PLACE!

BMM
AH...
THOK
KRK
THIS BODY IS AMAZING!
HWSH
AHAHA! LIMITLESS POWER!
TWRRRRRL
KOKO!
DGSHHHHHHH
KRMBL

HA HA HA
NO ONE CAN STOP ME NOW!
HA HA
HA HA HA HA
WHK
THWK
WE DON'T HAVE A CHANCE.
NO ONE CAN BEAT HIM IN THAT BODY.
IT'S HOPE-LESS...
A MARTIAL ARTS MASTER WITH MOKA'S POWER ...?!
WORST-CASE SCENARIO.
!!
I'M DISAP-POINTED...

DIDN'T YOU SWEAR TO DEFEAT ME SOMEDAY?
LOOK AT YOU...
HEH
HEH HEH
YOU'RE ALL TALK, HUH?
W-W...
...WHY...
...YOU...!
FWHH
DIE.
VWHH
...
OH...

G RIP
IT WORKED!
HF
HF
HF
FMP
HE'S BACK.
TSUKUNE!

HMPH. YOU AGAIN.
GN
TOO BAD...
ALL YOU HAD GOING FOR YOU WAS THAT GHOUL VIBE. NOW YOU'VE LOST IT...
NNH
ZSS
AND I'M MORE POWERFUL THAN ALL OF YOU PUT TOGETHER!
SHHHH
GK
!!
GH...
NH...
FSHHHH
NO ONE CAN STAND UP TO ME NOW.
I'M INVINCI-BLE!
DIE!
GRRP

WH... WHAT'S ...

BRR
BRR
BRR

...HAPPEN-ING?

MY POWER!

ALL MY POWER... EVAPORAT-ING!

SHHH

FWS

VAMPIRES ...
...APPEAR INVINCIBLE— BUT THEY'RE NOT.
THE TRUTH IS, THEIR POWER CAN BE QUITE EASILY CONTAINED...
...BY THIS ROSARIO, FOR INSTANCE.
THAT SEAL SHE WAS WEARING...!
YOU'RE NOT GOING TO HURT ANYONE ELSE.
ESPECIALLY NOT IN MOKA'S FORM.

YOU THINK YOU CAN KEEP THIS TRINKET ON ME?!
I'LL JUST RIP IT OFF AND—
YRNK
WHAT AN IDIOT.
YOU THINK WE'D JUST STAND AROUND AND LET YOU...?
WE'VE BEEN TRAINING...
...FOR SOMETHING JUST LIKE THIS...
INNER MOKA ATTACK

BLACK AND WHITE DUET #9
NO!
I CAN'T LOSE...
NOT TO... GIRLS!

FWIP
TOOOOOM
AFTER ALL, I'VE ELUDED CAPTURE A THOUSAND TIMES...
HF
HF
...FROM MUCH MORE FORMIDABLE OPPONENTS.

AND GOSH, LOOK! I'M INVINCIBLE AGAIN!
HUF...
NOW THAT I'M FREE OF THAT STUPID SEAL... YOU DON'T HAVE A CHANCE IN HELL!
HUF...

HATE TO BREAK IT TO YOU...
YOU'RE STRONG, NO DOUBT.
TA
BUT YOU'VE TAKEN ON A LOT OF DAMAGE FROM US...
?!!

YUP. PLUS YOU FORGOT SOMEBODY...
HOOO OOOOOO OOO

WHERE DO YOU THINK I GOT THIS ROSARIO FROM?
I TOOK IF OFF MOKA...TO RELEASE HER POWER.
CHLK

...
NO...

WHAT'S THE MATTER? YOU LOOK PALE.
I HOPE YOU DIDN'T SEE A DOPPELGÄNGER. BECAUSE, YOU KNOW... THAT MEANS YOU'RE GOING TO DIE.
HEH HEH HEH

TO
OOOOM

DON'T UNDER-ESTIMATE ME, YOU LITTLE BITCHES!
OOPS. YOU STUMBLED.
MAYBE *YOU'RE* THE ONE WHO UNDER-ESTIMATED *US!*

KNOW YOUR PLACE!

7: Gro-Gro Drops

Band of Thieves Captured!

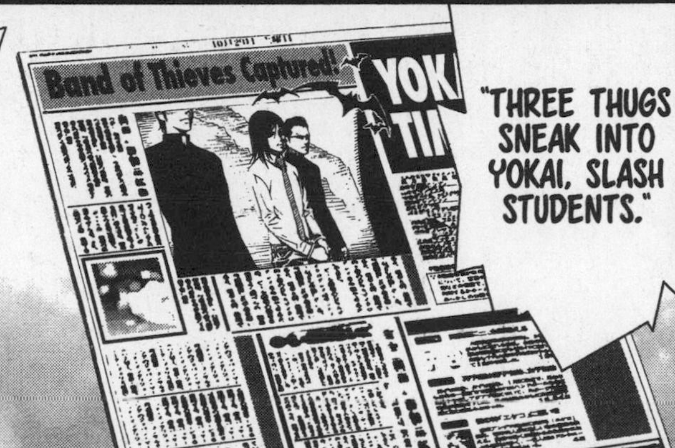

Band of Thieves Captured!
"THREE THUGS SNEAK INTO YOKAI, SLASH STUDENTS."
"ATTACKERS APPREHENDED AFTER DUNGEON SHOWDOWN."

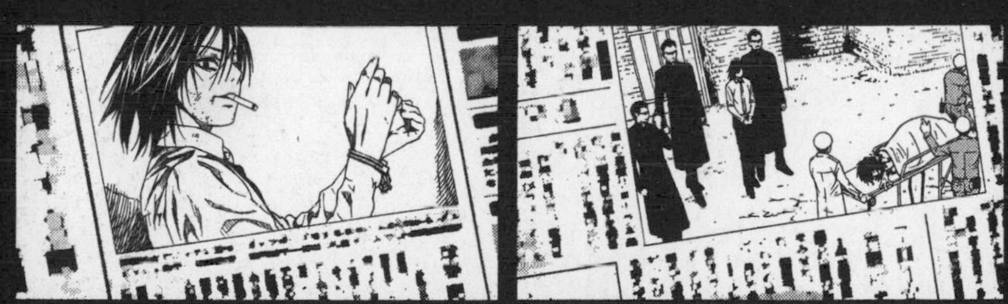

TWO DAYS LATER...
...LIFE IS BACK TO NORMAL AT YOKAI.
JUST ANOTHER BLIP IN A TEENAGER MONSTER'S SCHOOL DAYS!

FIRST ONE OF THE SCHOOL YEAR!

BRRING
News Club
KONG
CHEERS!
GREAT WORK!

WHEE! ♡
OUR NEWSPAPER'S A BEST SELLER AGAIN!
PHEW
I'M SO GLAD!

MAKES ALL THE HARD WORK WORTH IT!
MOKA, YOUR ILLUSTRATIONS ARE GREAT! AND SO IS YOUR LAYOUT, YUKARI!

TH-THANKS, TSUKUNE.
AW, SHUCKS.

HEY! TSUKUNE ...!
YOU DIDN'T LIKE MY COOKING CORNER?!
AHAHAHAHAHAHA
Tee-hee ... Tee-hee ...
OR MY SHORT STORY?

FLAP
HEY! WHAT'S THE BIG IDEA?
MY SISTER WAS THE ONE WHO DEFEATED THE BAD GUY!
BUT THERE ISN'T A WORD ABOUT THAT IN HERE!

THERE OUGHTA BE A FULL-PAGE SPREAD HIGHLIGHTING MOKA'S HEROICS!
MMMG
YOKAI TIMES
KEE!
AND HER BIG-SISTER COMPLEX REARS ITS UGLY HEAD AGAIN...

KOKO, THAT'S NOT THE POINT!
JOURNALISM ISN'T ABOUT GETTING CREDIT!
WHAT ARE YOU DOING HERE ANYWAY?

OH... WELL, I... UM...
!

DON'T TELL ME...

...YOU WANNA JOIN...
...THE NEWS CLUB!
?!!

YOU SHOULDA SAID SO RIGHT OFF! WE DON'T HAVE ANY FRESHMEN!
LOOM
AND WE NEED THE YOUNG FOLKS' POINT OF VIEW!

WAIT A MINUTE!!
POP
POP
POP
Welcome to the NEWS CLUB

I'M A PROUD VAMPIRE!
WHY WOULD I JOIN YOUR STUPID LITTLE—
...

SIGN ME UP.
SHAP
YEEK!

WELL, I NEVER OFFICIALLY ENROLLED, Y'KNOW...
OH, THAT'S RIGHT.
Club Enrollment
Year 2 Group 1 Mizore Shirayuki
Club: News
Reason to Join: Enjoy Teamwork, writing, and Tsukune.

MAY I JOIN AS WELL?
RUBY— YOU TOO?!
BUT, RUBY... YOU'RE NOT A STUDENT.

I GOT PERMISSION FROM THE HEAD-MASTER.
AS A REWARD FOR HELPING TO CATCH THOSE SLASHERS, HE'S APPOINTED ME AS THE CLUB'S ASSISTANT ADVISOR.
Club Enrollment
Year 2 Group 1 Ruby Tojo
Club: News
Reason to Join: Advisor

GO AHEAD! ORDER ME AROUND!
I LIVE TO SERVE!
NEVER HEARD OF GIVING ORDERS TO AN ADVISOR...

BUT WE'RE GLAD TO HAVE YOU! AND MIZORE!
KOKO TOO!
I JUST TOLD YOU, I'M NOT—
POPOP

WOK
WELCOME TO THE NEWS CLUB!
WHAT THE—?
SAKE
Catnip

M-MS. NEKONOME!! W-WHY ARE YOU DRESSED LIKE THAT?!!
AREN'T I CUTE? I FEEL THIRTY YEARS YOUNGER! ♡
THIRTY YEARS SUBTRACTED FROM...?
NewsPaper Club
MEEEEOW
NEW MEMBERS ARE ESSENTIAL FOR A CLUB'S GROWTH!
Sweet 16 again!
I'M PROUD TO TURN OUR NEWSPAPER OVER TO THE NEXT GENERATION!
IN FACT...
SINCE WE SEEM TO BE RIDING A WAVE...
LET'S GET OUT THERE RIGHT NOW AND DRUM UP SOME MORE NEW MEMBERS!
NOW?!
IN THE MIDDLE OF OUR PARTY ?!
YOU KNOW WHAT THEY SAY— STRIKE WHILE THE IRON IS HOT!
AA...?
WAIT JUST A—
WH
NO FAIR!!

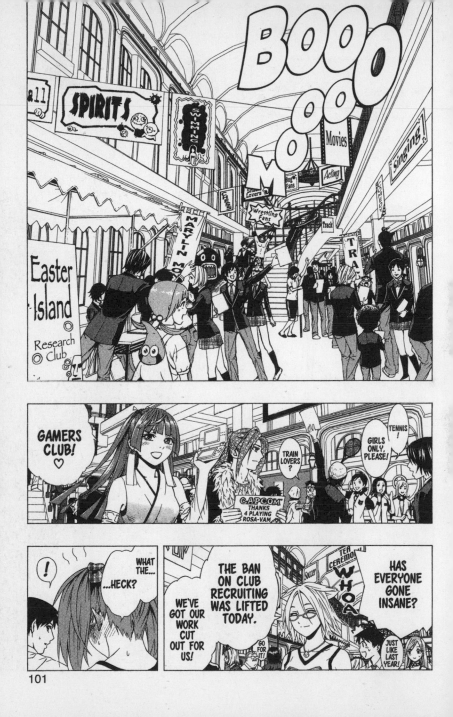

BOOOOOOM
Movies
Singing!
Acting
COMEDY
Track
TRA
Bug Fans
Wrestling Fans
CHESS
MARYLIN MO
SWIMMING
SPIRITS
Easter Island Research Club

WHY DO I HAVE TO WEAR THIS? I'M NOT A MEMBER OF YOUR DORKY CLUB!
AARRRRRH
I'M A PROUD VAMPIRE! NO VAMPIRE WOULD WEAR ANYTHING AS LAME AS—
LOOKS LIKE *ONE* WOULD...
BING
FOR SHAME! SHAME!
FOOOSH
Wanna be a reporter?
DON'T WORRY. IT LOOKS GOOD ON *YOU.*
WHAT GOOD IS PRIDE IF IT GETS IN THE WAY OF FUN?!
YOU CALL THIS FUN?!
BLUSH
ANYWAY, WHY WOULD ANYONE JOIN THE NEWS CLUB JUST BECAUSE WE'RE DRESSED LIKE—

HOTTIES!!!

BOOM

Enroll

I'M IN! I'M IN!

Enroll

Enroll

Enroll

NewsPaper Club

I'M NOT JOINING YOUR STUPID NEWS CLUB!!

KOKO!

Photo Club

WHO CARES ABOUT JOINING A CLUB ANYWAY ?!
I DON'T HAVE TIME FOR STUFF LIKE THAT!

RIGHT, BATTY?
PATA
PATA
YOU UNDER-STAND, DON'T YOU?
PATA

...
KIIII

NEWS CLUB... HMPH.
SURE, THE BATTLE IN THE DUNGEON WAS KINDA COOL, BUT...

HOW COME YOU...
...DON'T WANNA JOIN?
URK

BECAUSE I...I...

Y-YUKARI?!!
I'VE BEEN LOOKING ALL OVER FOR YOU.
WILL YOU JUST LEAVE ME ALONE?
I'M NOT JOINING YOUR PATHETIC CLUB.
TMP
HMMPH
I CAN'T LEAVE YOU ALONE.
AS YOUR ELDER, IT'S MY RESPONSIBILITY TO GUIDE YOU.
TP
SINCE WHEN ARE YOU MY ELDER?!
HEH HEH HEH
WELL, YOU'RE A FRESHMAN AND I'M A SOPHOMORE, RIGHT?
YEAH, BUT I'M OLDER THAN YOU!
GRADE TRUMPS AGE.
NNNNNGH
NOW, YOU LISTEN TO BIG SIS YUKARI AND...
HEY!
...
TP TP TP

I'M TRYING TO GUIDE YOU!
WHAT A PEST.
GLOM

LOOK, I DON'T HAVE TIME FOR THIS...
I HAVE TO CATCH UP TO MY REAL BIG SISTER.

BELIEVE ME, KOKO...
I GET IT. TOTAL-LY.

YOU SEE, I'M...
...JUST LIKE YOU.
BECAUSE I LOVE MOKA TOO.

Y-YOU ...?!!
MOKA IS SO STRONG, SO BEAUTIFUL, SO... PERFECT.
IT'S HARD ON THE LIKES OF US.
YUP YUP
YOU...
YOU REALLY GET IT?
YOU UNDER-STAND WHY I'VE GOT TO TOUGHEN UP?

SHE...

SKWIZ

SHE'LL DISOWN ME...

GASP
OH, COME ON, KOKO...

SEE?! I TOLD YOU!!
YOU CAN'T POSSIBLY UNDERSTAND HOW I FEEL!

YAAGH!
PSSSSH
sob sob
GASP!

KOKO, I DO UNDERSTAND. LIKE YOU, I LONG FOR THE DAY MOKA FINALLY ACKNOWL-EDGES ME.

Y-YOU DO?!

SOMETIMES, I FEEL SO CHILDISH THAT I CRY ALONE AT NIGHT.

YEAH. I GET THAT.

...

FWAP FWAP

I PUT MY HANDS ON MY HEART... AND THEN I CRY ALL THE MORE 'CAUSE I'M SO FLAT CHESTED!

OH YEAH. THAT TOO.

NO ONE ELSE UNDERSTANDS OUR PAIN! WE SHOULD JOIN FORCES!

YEAH! FORM A FLAT-CHESTED CLUB!

SHAKE

EXACTLY! EXCEPT WITHOUT THE SELF-HATING NAME...

RAAAH!
KOOOM

TEN GRAVESTONES AT ONCE!
OOOO
THAT'S GOTTA BE A RECORD!
THE KARATE CLUB ROCKS!

RABBL
IF YOU'RE LOOKIN' FOR A GOOD TIME, JOIN THE JUDO CLUB!
RABBL
NO, SIGN UP FOR KICK-BOXING!
No, no!

WHERE ARE WE...?
THE MARTIAL ARTS PAVILION.
IF YOU WANT TO TOUGHEN UP, THESE ARE THE CLUBS FOR YOU!
HUH?!

THE MARTIAL ARTS PROGRAM IS SUPPOSED TO BE ONE OF YOKAI'S GREATEST STRENGTHS.

AND KURUMU AND MIZORE TRAIN IN THE MARTIAL ARTS, YOU KNOW.

THEY DO...?

SO... YOU'RE NOT GONNA TRY TO CONVINCE ME TO JOIN THE NEWS CLUB?
I WOULDN'T PRESSURE YOU TO DO ANYTHING YOU DON'T WANT TO DO.
But I'd love it if you joined!
...
I ALWAYS THOUGHT MARTIAL ARTS WAS JUST FOR FUN... BUT IF IT'LL TOUGHEN ME UP...

I GUESS...
...IT MIGHT BE WORTH A TRY.

NO WAY!
HEE HEE

THIS CLUB IS *SERIOUS.*
IT'S NO PLACE FOR LITTLE GIRLS.
GONG
WHAT ...?
THAT'S SEXIST!
IT'S NOT BECAUSE YOU'RE GIRLS. IT'S BECAUSE YOU'RE *LITTLE.*

HYAH!
BING
KRAK

TEN GRAVESTONES AGAIN! THIS CLUB IS THE BOMB!
COME BACK AFTER YOU CAN BREAK AT LEAST *ONE* OF THOSE.
HEE HEE HEE
ONE ...?

YOU THINK I CAN'T?!
GIMME A TURN AND I'LL—
ARGH

THAT'LL BE 1,000 YEN.
GRAVE-STONE CHOPPING

BUT IF YOU BREAK MORE IN ONE GO THAN HE CAN, YOU WIN 5,000 YEN. (LIMITED TIME OFFER.)
HEEEE
TEE HEE
LET'S TRY SOME OTHER CLUBS.
HOOOO

NO WAY. YOU GIRLS WOULD GET KILLED.
THAI BOXING
TOSS

Wrestling
COME BACK WHEN YOU'RE A WHOLE LOT TALLER!
TOSS

SUMO
TOSS

WHY DO THEY ALL SAY I'M JUST A KID?!

NO FAIR!!

WAAAAAAAAA

MAGICAL ...
...GRO-GRO DROPS!
TAAAAAA
DAAAAAA
INSTANT MATURITY!
GRO-GRO DROPS?!
YUP! MAGIC CANDY I CONJURED UP JUST FOR OCCASIONS LIKE THIS!
SWALLOW ONE AND YOU'LL INSTANTLY ...
...WELL, THEORET-ICALLY... I MEAN, UH... ACTUALLY I HAVEN'T TESTED IT YET.
Gulp
MIND BEING...
...MY GUINEA PIG?

COME ONE, COME ALL!
NO MORE CHALLENG-ERS?!
OOOOO
OOO
THE RECORD'S SET AT *TEN* STONES!
BEAT THAT AND WIN YERSELF 5,000 YEN!

MGH!
AWW, TOO BAD... THAT'LL BE 1,000 YEN, THANKS!
GONK
AHA HA HA HA
Y'ALL COME BACK SOON NOW!
KRAK
KRAK

HEE HEE... THEY DON'T STAND A CHANCE...
SNICKER
'CAUSE WE GIVE CHALLENGERS EXTRA HARD STONES!

HEH... YOU'RE A CLEVER ONE!
HEE HEE HEE
WE AREN'T GETTING ANY NEW MEMBERS... BUT WE SURE ARE RAKING IN THE DOUGH!

TMP
I'LL TAKE YOUR CHALLENGE.
BUT I'LL PAY THE 1,000 YEN LATER.
HUH...?
NO WAY! YOU CAN'T PAY AFTER-WARDS!

FLIP
KSSSH
KSSSH
NewsPaPer Club
WSSSH
GASP GASP
GASP
SSSSS
WH-WHO IS THAT?
WHY DON'T I RECOGNIZE A MEMBER OF THE STUDENT BODY WITH THAT BODY?
YAMA YAMA
OH, SHE'S ABOUT TO...
YAMA YAMA
...K-K-KARATE CHOP! ♡
NewsPaPer Club
...

DOOO
!!!!
OOOOM
FWIP
THIR-TEEN STONES! A NEW RECORD!
BZZ
BZZ
BZZ

I CAN'T BELIEVE IT! SHE DID IT!
OOOOO
SHE BROKE OUR RECORD!
SHE'S HOT AND POWERFUL!
WHAT A BABE!
...
WOW ...
OOOOOOO
SO WHAT'S YOUR NAME?
DO YOU HAVE A BOY-FRIEND?
YOU'RE RIGHT. I WON'T PAY LATER.
GRIN
I'LL JUST TAKE THAT PRIZE MONEY NOW. ♡

YAHOO!
CLAP
YOUR MAGIC GRO-GRO CANDIES WORKED!

DID YOU HEAR THOSE GUYS TALKING ABOUT ME JUST NOW?!
I'M NOT ONLY POWERFUL, I'M HOT! ♡
THIS IS GREAT!
IF YOU'RE HAPPY, I'M HAPPY!
Plus, I got research data and money!

I HAD NO IDEA IT WAS SO FUN TO BE A GROWN-UP!
MY BODY'S BURSTING WITH POWER, MY LINE OF SIGHT IS HIGHER... THIS IS A DREAM COME TRUE!
AND CHECK OUT THESE!

AREN'T THEY AWE-SOME?
GOOB
YEP! AWESOME!
THEY'RE ...
...HUMON-GOUS!
WOBBL OBBL OBBL
AMAZING! TRULY AMAZING!
STARE
WOBBL
WOWWIE!

YEP, YOU'RE AMAZING, ALL RIGHT!
!!
YEEK!
YOU REALLY SURPRISED US, UH-HUH.
ZA
C'MON! YOU GOTTA JOIN OUR CLUB!

NO THANKS.

YOU GUYS ARE TOO WIMPY FOR ME.

HMPH

SS
SSSSSHH
FLIP FLIP

ONE... PUNCH. ONE... P-PUNCH...
SNIF SNIF
THE SHAME...

YOU'RE MOKA'S SISTER ALL RIGHT!
WOW
I FEEL AWESOME!
LIKE I'M OVER-FLOWING WITH POWER!

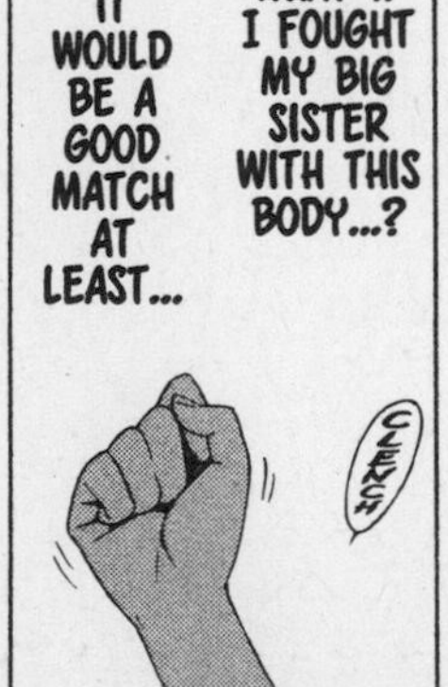
WHAT IF I FOUGHT MY BIG SISTER WITH THIS BODY...?
IT WOULD BE A GOOD MATCH AT LEAST...
CLENCH

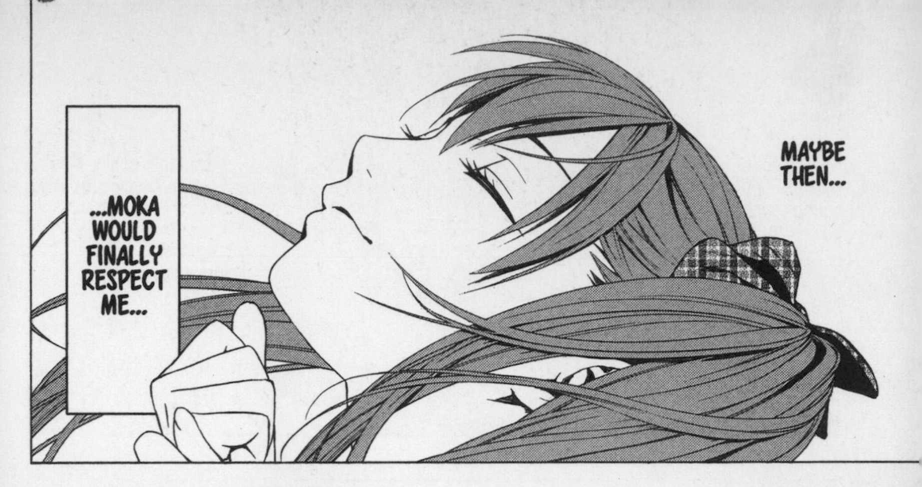
MAYBE THEN...
...MOKA WOULD FINALLY RESPECT ME...

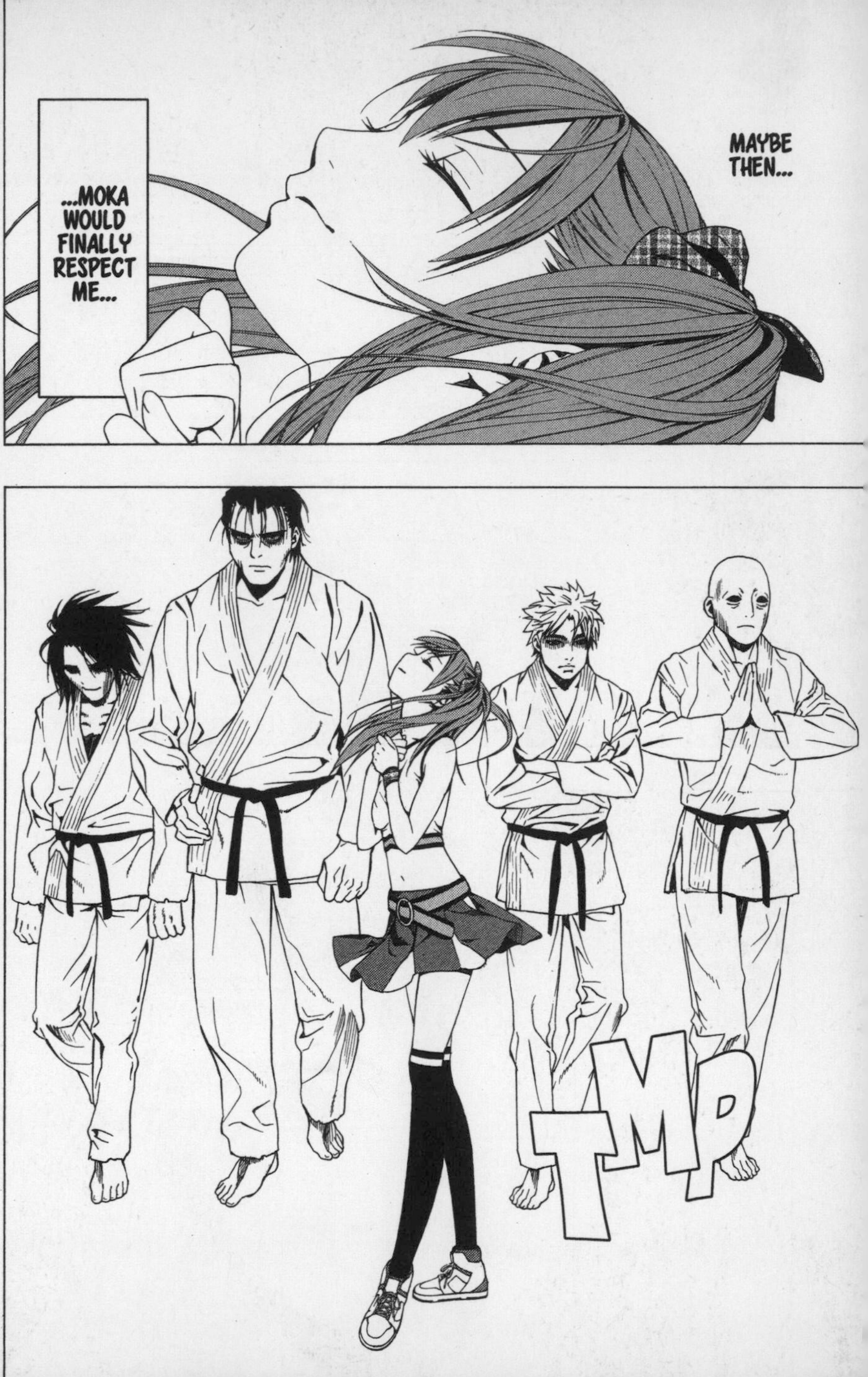

TMP

OKAY, FINE.

IF YOU BEAT ME, I'LL JOIN YOUR CLUB.

I LIKE YOUR SPIRIT, GIRL.
HA! LET'S DO THIS, BATTY!
KIII
FSSH
FSSH
!
POOF
NewsPaper Club

...

HUH...?
BRRR

HOW'D HE GET SO BIG ALL OF A SUDDEN?
NOT TO MEN-TION...
...
PSS PSS

WHAT DO YOU MEAN I GOT SMALLER?!
THAT'S RIDICU-LOUS!

I'M NOT...
YAAAAAAAAA!!
KABOOOM
NewsPaper Club

GASP
DOOOOOM
KRAK KRAK
To be continued

MEAN-WHILE, BACK AT THE BOOTH...
WHERE D'YOU SUPPOSE KOKO AND YUKARI WENT OFF TO?
I HOPE THEY'RE NOT GETTING INTO TROUBLE...
SLOG SLOG SLOG SLOG
EVERYONE WHO WANTS TO JOIN THE NEWS CLUB, FORM A LINE OVER HERE, PLEASE!
How many reporters do we need?
As usual...

8: The Fearsome Kids

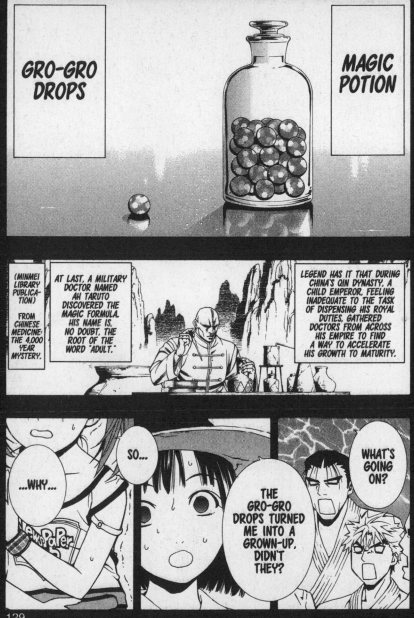

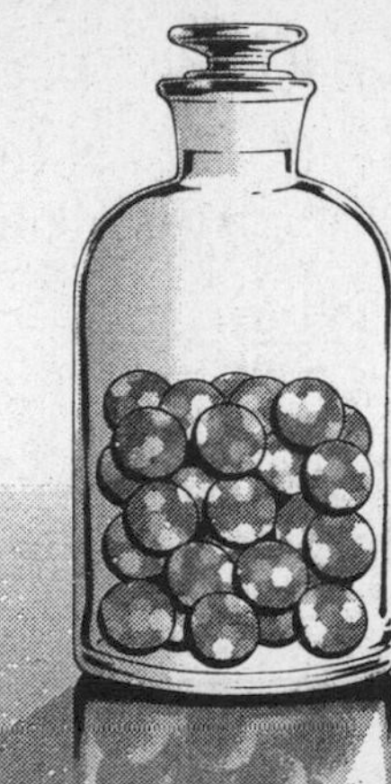
MAGIC POTION
GRO-GRO DROPS

LEGEND HAS IT THAT DURING CHINA'S QIN DYNASTY, A CHILD EMPEROR, FEELING INADEQUATE TO THE TASK OF DISPENSING HIS ROYAL DUTIES, GATHERED DOCTORS FROM ACROSS HIS EMPIRE TO FIND A WAY TO ACCELERATE HIS GROWTH TO MATURITY.
AT LAST, A MILITARY DOCTOR NAMED AH TARUTO DISCOVERED THE MAGIC FORMULA. HIS NAME IS, NO DOUBT, THE ROOT OF THE WORD "ADULT."
(MINMEI LIBRARY PUBLICATION)
FROM CHINESE MEDICINE: THE 4,000 YEAR MYSTERY.

WHAT'S GOING ON?
SO...
THE GRO-GRO DROPS TURNED ME INTO A GROWN-UP, DIDN'T THEY?
...WHY...

...AM I...EVEN YOUNGER NOW THAN I USED TO BE?!
CHBIH
Normally 4'11"
After Gro-Gro Drops 5'4"
Currently 3'11"
REBOUND?
TURN ME BACK TO NORMAL!
I...DON'T KNOW HOW! I'LL NEED SOME TIME TO FIGURE OUT HOW TO REVERSE THIS SIDE EFFECT.
SORRY. I GUESS THAT'S WHAT YOU GET...
AHA HA HA
...FOR TRYING UNTESTED POTIONS!

ALL I WANTED WAS TO BE TOUGH...

...TO CATCH UP WITH MY MAGNIFI-CENT SISTER.
AND NOW I'VE FALLEN EVEN FURTHER BEHIND!
WHAT IF SHE...

...SEES ME LIKE THIS?!

I'VE GOT TO GET MY REGULAR BODY BACK—AND FAST!

I CAN'T LET HER SEE ME THIS...PUNY! I COULDN'T STAND IT!

BRRR

BRRR

TMP

HMPH.

WHY'D YOU HAVE TO GO AND SHRINK NOW?

WE'RE IN THE MIDDLE OF A DUEL!

EEP!

YOU THINK TURNING INTO A KID...
KRAK KRAK KRAK
...IS AN EXCUSE TO FORFEIT?

HEE HEE... THAT'S TELLING HER, HAIJI!
!
SHE FIGHTS DIRTY! SHE CAUGHT US WITH A SNEAK ATTACK!
STUMBLE
SHRINKING IS JUST ANOTHER TRICK!
SHOW HER HOW KARATE MASTERS TEACH DIRTY FIGHTERS A LESSON!

HYUU
BOM
HOOOOOOOOOO
BRAK

KARATE CLUB CAPTAIN HAIJI MIYAMOTO.
I'LL TEACH YOU TO RESPECT KARATE!

SHHHHHH

TH-THAT BLOW...
I...I COULDN'T EVEN SEE IT!

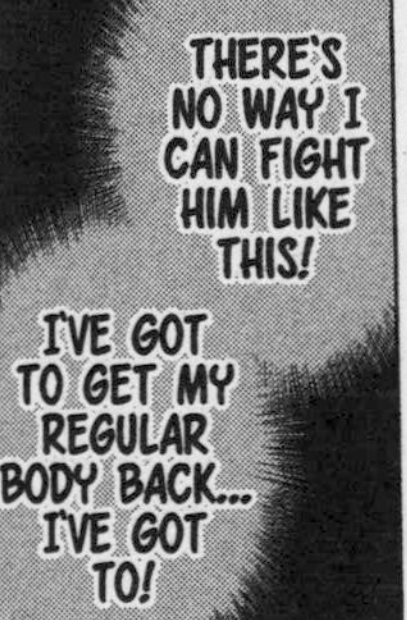
THERE'S NO WAY I CAN FIGHT HIM LIKE THIS!
I'VE GOT TO GET MY REGULAR BODY BACK... I'VE GOT TO!

Heh

PAT
JUST KIDDING!
I COULD NEVER HIT YOU.
HA HA HA HA
YOU'RE SUCH A CUTIE.
PAT PAT
TO TELL THE TRUTH, I JUST WUVS WIDDLE KIDDIES!
...

AS FOR YOU TWO—QUIT SPAZZING OUT BECAUSE A GIRL BEAT YOU!
LET'S GO.
HUH? N-NO!
CAP-TAIN...!

HOLD ON A SEC! ARE YOU SAYING...
...I'M NOT EVEN WORTH FIGHTING?!

HAHAHA! ♡ LITTLE GIRL, YOU ARE TOTALLY ADORA-BUBBLE!
WHEE! WHEE!
AGH! QUIT IT! PUT ME DOWN!
AND QUIT CALLING ME "LITTLE"!
WANNA WRESTLE? ♡
THIS IS HOW YOU SHOW YOUR "WUV"?!

CAREFUL, HAIJI!
GOO GOO GA-GA

SHE MIGHT LOOK CUTE, BUT SHE'S EVIL!
KII KII
AVENGE OUR HONOR!
BEAT HER TO A PULP!
...

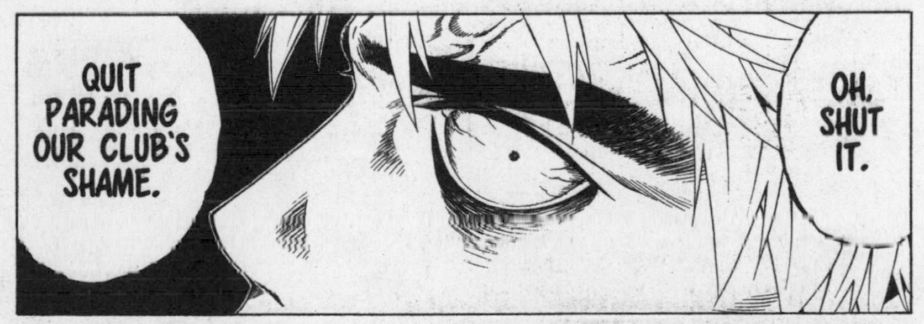
OH, SHUT IT.
QUIT PARADING OUR CLUB'S SHAME.

BRRRR
PWIK

LET'S GO.
Y-YES, SIR...
...
EEK!

GNH

K-KOKO! WE'RE SAVED!
LET'S GET BACK TO THE NEWS CLUB ROOM BEFORE WE ATTRACT ANY MORE ATTENTION.

YOU CALL THAT SAVED ?!
I'D RATHER GET POUNDED THAN HUMILI-ATED!!
IN THEIR EYES, WE WEREN'T EVEN WORTH FIGHTING!
WAGH!

I CAN'T GO BACK TO THE NEWS CLUB LIKE THIS!
ONE LOOK AT ME AND EVERYONE'S GONNA BUST OUT LAUGHING!
BUT WHERE ELSE CAN WE GO?
NO! I WON'T LET THEM SEE ME THIS WAY! UH-UH!
Pink

NEWS CLUB...
...
GNNN

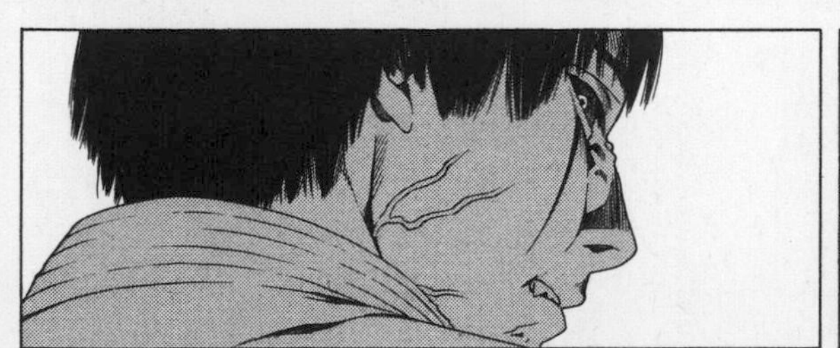

RABBL
RABBL
RABBL

GRO-GRO DROPS, HUH?
CANDY THAT AGES THE USER...
Wa hah!
Hah!
Hah!
BAM BAM
BAM BAM
BAM BAM
hoo hoo hoo
Brilliant work, Yukari!
BAM BAM
THE MAGIC CANDY AUGMENTS YOUR NATURAL TRANSFORMATIVE POWERS, KOKO...
SO YOU SHOULD CHANGE BACK... EVENTUALLY...
...

OH, PLEASE DON'T!!
YOU'RE SO CUTE THIS WAY!
SMALLER SUITS YOU.
PAT PAT
KURUMU! MIZORE!
Don't tease her!

WHY DID YOU WANT TO BE OLDER ANYWAY?
ANY SPECIAL REASON?

W-WELL... WHEN I TRIED TO JOIN THE KARATE CLUB, THEY MADE FUN OF ME, AND...AND...

I THOUGHT YOU WERE JOINING THE NEWS CLUB.
I DIDN'T SAY ANY SUCH THING!

YOU'LL REGRET IT IF YOU DON'T.
WE'RE THE HOTTEST CLUB AT SCHOOL NOW!

WE GOT SO MANY APPLICANTS THAT...
SIGH
I love Moka!
WANNABES
I love Kurumu!
hee hee!
...WE HAD TO SCHEDULE A LOTTERY TOMORROW.
WHY ARE THEY ALL GUYS?! CREEPY-LOOKING GUYS, AT THAT!

IF YOU COMMIT TONIGHT, YOU WON'T HAVE TO GO THROUGH THE LOTTERY.
YOU CAN BE OUR MASCOT!
QUIT MESSING WITH MY HEAD!
I'D RATHER BE DEAD THAN A MASCOT!
RUB RUB
RUB RUB
KIIII
DAMMIT! EVERYBODY'S MAKING FUN OF ME...
I'M A PROU—
I'M A PROUD VAMPIRE!
RUB RUB
RUB
AGH!

DON'T LAUGH AT HER.

HMPH

SHE ONLY *LOOKS* LIKE A KID. KOKO IS STILL KOKO.

WE SHOULD TREAT HER THE SAME AS USUAL.

WHERE ARE WE?
THE CRAFT CLUB'S ROOM.
UM ...
MAY WE BORROW SOME COSTUMES? IN KIDS' SIZES?
SURE ...

HERE. WEAR THESE UNTIL YOU GET BACK TO NORMAL.
I THINK THEY'LL SUIT YOU.
MY BIG SIS...

SNIF

NO ONE ELSE...
...TAKES ME SERI-OUSLY...

BUT SHE GETS ME.
THERE'S NOTHING LIKE A SISTER...
...
PFFT
GONG
WHAT ARE YOU DOING?!
ARRRR
WHAT AM I, A PRE-SCHOOLER?!
BUT IT LOOKS SO CUTE ON YOU!
I CAN'T WEAR THIS!
IT'S A PERFECT FIT!
HITS YOU SMACK-DAB IN THE MATERNAL INSTINCTS, HUH?
AHAHAHA HA
IT FITS MY BODY BUT NOT MY DIGNITY!
HA HA HA
MAYBE SOMETHING A LITTLE MORE CASUAL WOULD WORK BETTER.
RUBY...?
HUF HUF

HOW ABOUT THESE OVERALLS?

*N-CHA

OH YEAH. THESE ARE GREAT.

I'LL JUST PUT THESE ON, STICK OUT MY ARMS AND GO KIIIIIN.

*Arale from *Dr. Slump* by Akira Toriyama

WHAT IS THIS, COSPLAY?!

I THOUGHT KIDS LOVED COSTUMES.

I'M NOT A KID!!

I HATE YOU!

WHAT ABOUT THIS?

BOOM

OH BOY. I GET TO BE A BABY AGAIN.

...

BOOM

PERFECT. WHAT CLUB DOESN'T NEED A BEAR?

OOOO! ♡ THIS ONE'S TOTALLY ADORABLE!
SIGH
IS THIS WHAT IT'LL BE LIKE WHEN TSUKUNE AND I HAVE CHILDREN?

...
HEH HEH
COME HOME WITH ME. I'LL RAISE YOU.

HEY! SHE'S MY BABY! MINE AND TSU-KUNE'S!
NO! MINE AND TSU-KUNE'S.
LET ME GO!!
...
STARE
HEY, I MADE COFFEE!
LET'S TAKE A BREAK.
ZHP
SIS! SAVE ME!
OH!
TSK...

NONE OF YOU UNDERSTAND HOW HUMILIATING IT IS TO BE DRESSED LIKE THIS!
NO ONE!
EXCEPT FOR YOU, RIGHT...?! YOU GET IT?!

OF COURSE. YOU'RE MY DEAR LITTLE SISTER.
NO ONE COULD POSSIBLY UNDERSTAND YOU LIKE I DO.

SKWEEZ
I KNEW IT!

RELAX, KOKO... HAVE A SEAT.
YOU'LL FEEL BETTER AFTER A LITTLE BREATHER.
KCHK
O-OKAY...

HERE YOU GO, EVERYBODY.
YUKARI, YOU WANT COFFEE TOO, RIGHT?
Thanks!

AND FOR YOU, KOKO— A YUMMY CREAM SODA!

YAY! ♡ I LOVE CREAM!

I CAN'T TAKE IT ANYMORE!!
ZIP
YAAAAA!
SPURT

SOB SOB

SOB SOB

KOKO...?

ARE YOU CRYING AGAIN?

I C-CAN'T...

...HELP IT...

KAHLUA AND THE OTHERS TREAT ME LIKE A LITTLE KID...

AND IT'S NOT JUST OUR SISTERS!

DAD AND MOM...

THEY TREAT ME LIKE—

BOOT

WH-WHADJA DO THAT FOR?!

CRYBABY!

IF YOU HAVE TIME TO CRY, YOU HAVE TIME TO *TRAIN.*

TOUGHEN UP, KOKO!
THAT'S THE ONLY WAY YOU'LL GET TAKEN SERIOUSLY IN THIS HOUSEHOLD.
YOU AND ME BOTH.
SHUT UP! I CAN KICK YOUR BUTT!
OH YEAH? TRY IT...
DONK
KOOM
DIE!!
BOK
GONG
KOOM KOOM
...
YOU DON'T PULL ANY PUNCHES, DO YOU?
SHHHH
'COURSE NOT.
IT ISN'T REAL TRAINING IF WE DON'T GO ALL OUT.
...
HOW COME ...
...YOU'RE THE ONLY ONE...
...WHO DOESN'T TREAT ME LIKE A BABY?

...
BECAUSE I'M A KID TOO.

IT'S TRUE. AND SHE'S ALL I'VE GOT.
KILL
I HATE...
...YOU...

I HATE ALL OF YOU!

TMP
I DON'T KNOW WHO YOU'RE YELLIN' AT...
BUT LOOKS LIKE YOU'RE HAVING A HARD TIME STUCK IN THAT KID'S BODY.

SERVES YOU RIGHT.

?!!

THOSE GRO-GRO DROPS...
HOW LONG TILL SHE'S NORMAL AGAIN?

I DON'T KNOW. WHY?
BECAUSE IF THIS LITTLE KOKO VS. BIG MOKA THING KEEPS UP...
...SHE'LL NEVER FORGIVE ME!
HUH?

KOKO ...
...IS THE YOUNGEST. OUR OLDER SISTERS ALWAYS MADE FUN OF HER.
I'd forgotten...
SHE WAS ALWAYS CRYING... SHE SAID OUR PARENTS HAD LOW EXPECTATIONS OF HER TOO.

HOW COULD I HAVE FORGOTTEN ALL THAT...AND TREATED HER LIKE THE BABY OF THE FAMILY AGAIN?

I THINK I REALLY HURT HER FEELINGS.

WHOOSH
GUH
WHOA! THIS KID'S FAST!
GRAB HER, YOU IDIOT!
IF WE GANG UP ON HER—
HOOSH
GAGA
GAGA
GRAH!
AAGH!

EVEN TOGETHER YOU GUYS AREN'T MUCH OF A THREAT.
IF YOU'RE GONNA BEAT ME UP, YOU'LL HAVE TO BRING ALONG THAT DORKY CAPTAIN OF YOURS.

IS SH-SHE REALLY JUST A KID...?
HE SAID SHE'D BE EASY PICKINGS! THIS ISN'T ANY FUN!
WHAT SHOULD WE—?

HEY!! HE'S GONE!!
YAMA YAMA
YOU'RE KIDDING! HE TOOK OFF?!
I CAN'T BELIEVE THAT GUY!!
...
HE RAN AWAY?
THE GUY WITH THE BOWL-SHAPED HEAD?
YADA YADA
HUF HUF
LUCKY FOR ME, BECAUSE THIS BODY ISN'T VERY STRONG...
I'D BETTER RUN FOR IT...
...BEFORE IT'S TOO...
BWK

HEE HEEHEE! IDIOT!
BONNNNG
I TOLD YOU! THIS ISN'T A KARATE MATCH!
AND I DIDN'T RUN AWAY...
GRIP
AAAH!

MY HOME IS UNDERGROUND.
ALL THAT CHATTER WAS PRETTY ANNOYING, BUT UP CLOSE... SHE'S QUITE A CATCH!
SHOOOOOO
BWK
MWK
BWK
WHOA!
SUPER SNEAK ATTACK!
DON'T THINK I'LL CUT YOU A BREAK 'CAUSE YOU'RE A KID.
Hee hee hee
YOW!
...
YOU PLAY DIRTIER THAN ANY GROWN-UP!
FR-FROM... UNDERGROUND ...?
D-DON'T HAVE...THE STRENGTH... TO FEND HIM OFF...
READY NOW...?
SWK
LET'S PLAY... TILT-A-GIRL!
I DON'T HAVE A CHANCE!
HE'S TOO STRONG!
NO...

NOOOOO!
RRRRR
RRR
RRRRRIP
HEE...
THUK
PLUP
...
!
WH... WHAT'S THIS...
...IN MY... FOREHEAD?

WH
MP
?!!
WH-WHO'S THROWING CARDS AT ME?!
WHAT VICIOUS...?
SHHHHHHHH
HUH? NO WAY...
WHAT ARE YOU...?
I CAME TO HELP...
...KOKO.

YU... YUKARI?!!
YOU ATE THE GRO-GRO CANDY TOO...?
GASP
Newspaper club
WSH
HOW COME? DID YOU TURN INTO A GROWN-UP TO MOCK ME?
FORGET IT!
I DON'T WANT YOUR STUPID HELP!

POOF
WHA... WHA... WHA...?
TWELVE MINUTES, THIRTEEN SECONDS.
THAT'S HOW LONG THE GRO-GRO DROPS TRANSFORM YOU INTO AN ADULT...BEFORE THE BACKLASH TURNS YOU INTO A KID.
Side effect.
WOK
AGH! WHAT DID YOU...?!
GAH!
AGH!
WHAT DO YOU THINK?
ARE WE EVEN NOW?
YEAH!
GREAT IDEA, MOKA!
WE CAN'T TREAT KOKO LIKE A KID ANYMORE...

...BECAUSE...
TOOM
TOOM
THEY'RE ALL LIKE ME!
EVERY ONE OF THEM TURNED INTO A LITTLE KID!
YEEE!

TOOM
...WE'RE ALL KIDS NOW!
HYAH!
LET'S GO!
C'MON, LET'S GET THOSE BIG JERKS!
THEY DID THIS... FOR ME?
...

...THIS GANG OF LITTLE GIRLS...

...IS ON THE RAMPAGE ?!!

OVER THERE!!
IT'S HIM!!
THE KARATE CLUB MEANIE!!
YEEEEE
HUH? ME?
I ONLY TEASE KIDS 'CAUSE I LOVES 'EM...
GET HIM!!
NO MERCY!!
AAA
WAIT! WAIT! WAIT!
WHY ARE THE LITTLE GIRLS...
...AT-TACKING ME?!
WHAT'D I DO?
I NEVER MET 'EM BEFORE IN MY LIFE!
DIE !!
AND...
...THEY'RE SO...
...CUTE! ♡
BLUSH

SUPER COMBO

KIDDIE ASSAULT !!

WE ARE...

...THE NEWS CLUB!

TOOOM

"NEWS CLUB DECIMATES KARATE CLUB"!
THIS STORY RACED THROUGH THE SCHOOL LIKE WILDFIRE...

...AND SOON BECAME LEGEND.
?!

AND SO...
HE HE
UM... WE'RE NOT GONNA JOIN THE NEWS CLUB AFTER ALL.

YOU'RE NOT?
HOW COME?!
ZOOM
'CAUSE WE DON'T WANNA GET EATEN!!

APPLICANTS—ZERO.
HOOO OOO
Applicants:
0
zero
BUT WE'RE SO NICE...
WHAT DO WE DO NOW?
FOLD, THAT'S WHAT.
CLUB RECRUIT-MENT—FAIL.
...

BUT...
LOOKS LIKE YOU'RE IN TROUBLE.
NEED SOME HELP?
FZH
!

I MEAN, IF YOU INSIST...
I GUESS I'D BE WILLING...
...TO JOIN YOUR CLUB.
Enrollment Form

YOU...
YOU MEAN IT?!

AND SO...
THE NEWS CLUB WELCOMES ANOTHER VALUABLE MEMBER.
BLUSH
Y'KNOW, IF YOU WANTED TO JOIN US, YOU COULD'VE JUST SAID SO IN THE FIRST PLACE!
BUT I DIDN'T!
YOU NEED TO WORK ON YOUR LYING...
WEL-COME, KOKO!
POPOP
Club Enrollment
ear 1 Group 5 Koko Shuzen
Club: News
Reason to Join:

MAGICAL CANDY [The End]

ROSARIO+VAMPIRE

Season II

SO... THE WORD "ADULT" COMES FROM CHINA?!

R-REALLY ?!!

Just like golf and ping-pong!

Library Publications

Minmei

ROSARIO + VAMPIRE

Season II

Meaningless End-of-Volume Theater

II

• Uncompromising #1 •

• Uncomprising #2 •

Please send questions and fan letters to ➡ Rosario+Vampire Fan Mail, VIZ Media, P.O. Box 77010, San Francisco, CA 94107

• Batty's Secret #1 •

BATTY, MY TRANS-FORMER BAT. (♂)
HE CAN TRANSFORM INTO ANY WEAPON HE'S SEEN.

BATTY IS SO CUTE!
I'VE ALWAYS WANTED A PET THAT COULD PERCH ON ME!
WOULD YOU LIKE HIM ON YOUR HEAD?
SERI-OUSLY?!

CAREFUL, THOUGH. HE'S SMALL, BUT HIS MASS IS THE SAME AS WHEN HE'S WEAPONIZED.
THE LAW OF CONSTANT MASS
FLAP
FLAP
?

HE WEIGHS 220 POUNDS.
HEAVY!
WHAM
YEAH, MY NECK GETS STIFF IF HE PERCHES ON ME TOO MUCH.

• Batty's Secret #2 •

TRANS-FORMER BATS ARE USUALLY A LOT BIGGER.
VEEP
HIS CHIBI FORM IS ONLY TEMPORARY.

TEMPO-RARY?!!
BUT I'VE ONLY SEEN HIM LIKE THIS. HE DOESN'T LIKE CHANGING BACK.

I'D LIKE TO SEE BATTY'S REAL FORM. ♡
GASP

MUNCH
MUNCH

Rosario+Vampire

Akihisa Ikeda

• Staff •

Makoto Saito
Kenji Tashiro
Nobuyuki Hayashi

• Help •

Hajime Maeda
Hirotaka Inoue
Shinichi Miyashita

• 3DCG •

Takaharu Yoshizawa

• Editing •

Makoto Watanabe

• Comic •

Kenju Noro

BE SURE TO READ VOLUME 3...

Check these out!

NEXT VOLUME
BRRRR
YOU BETTER HURRY UP AND MAKE SOME BABY SNOW FAIRIES!
GRIN
Mizore's mother turns up the pressure!
THE ENTIRE NEWS CLUB IS INVITED TO THE LAND OF THE SNOW FAIRIES !!
YAY! VACATION!
SWH
STEP ON IT, BUS DRIVER!

On the eve of her 17th birthday, what does Mizore want from Tsukune...?!
!
SWH
TSUKUNE, COME HERE AND...
ROSARIO+VAMPIRE
Season II
presented by Akihisa Ikeda
ROSARIO+VAMPIRE: SEASON II, VOL. 3
ON SALE DECEMBER 2010!!

AKIHISA IKEDA

Thank you for picking up this manga. This is the second volume of "Rosa-Vam" Season II.

Looking back, Season I told the story of the main character, Tsukune, growing up. Because he was the focus, I didn't have room to draw a lot of episodes about his friends that I wanted to do. From this volume on, I'm going to include those stories... and it's going to be fun!

If Season I was the story of Tsukune, then Season II is the story of his friends. They're going to really get the party going! Have fun reading!

Akihisa Ikeda was born in 1976 in Miyazaki. He debuted as a mangaka with the four-volume magical warrior fantasy series *Kiruto* in 2002, which was serialized in *Monthly Shonen Jump*. *Rosario+Vampire* debuted in *Monthly Shonen Jump* in March of 2004 and is continuing in the magazine *Jump Square (Jump SQ)* as *Rosario+Vampire: Season II*. In Japan, *Rosario+Vampire* is also available as a drama CD. In 2008, the story was released as an anime. Season II is also available as an anime now. And in Japan, there is a Nintendo DS game based on the series.

Ikeda has been a huge fan of vampires and monsters since he was a little kid. He says one of the perks of being a manga artist is being able to go for walks during the day when everybody else is stuck in the office.

ROSARIO+VAMPIRE: Season II

2

SHONEN JUMP ADVANCED Manga Edition

STORY & ART BY AKIHISA IKEDA

Translation/Kaori Inoue
English Adaptation/Gerard Jones
Touch-up Art & Lettering/Stephen Dutro
Cover & Interior Design/Hidemi Sahara
Editor/Annette Roman

VP, Production/Alvin Lu
VP, Sales & Product Marketing/Gonzalo Ferreyra
VP, Creative/Linda Espinosa
Publisher/Hyoe Narita

Printed in the U.S.A.

Published by VIZ Media, LLC
P.O. Box 77010
San Francisco, CA 94107

10 9 8 7 6 5 4 3 2 1
First printing, August 2010

www.viz.com

www.shonenjump.com

PARENTAL ADVISORY
ROSARIO+VAMPIRE is rated T+ for Older Teen and is recommended for ages 16 and up. It contains suggestive situations and violence.

ratings.viz.com

CRYPT SHEET FOR

ROSARIO+VAMPIRE: SEASON II, VOL. 3

SNOW ORACLE

TEST 3

WHEN MAGICAL WARMING STRIKES YOKAI ACADEMY, YOU HAD BETTER...

a. reduce your supernatural footprint

b. hightail it to snow-fairy country

c. deny that monster activity has anything to do with it

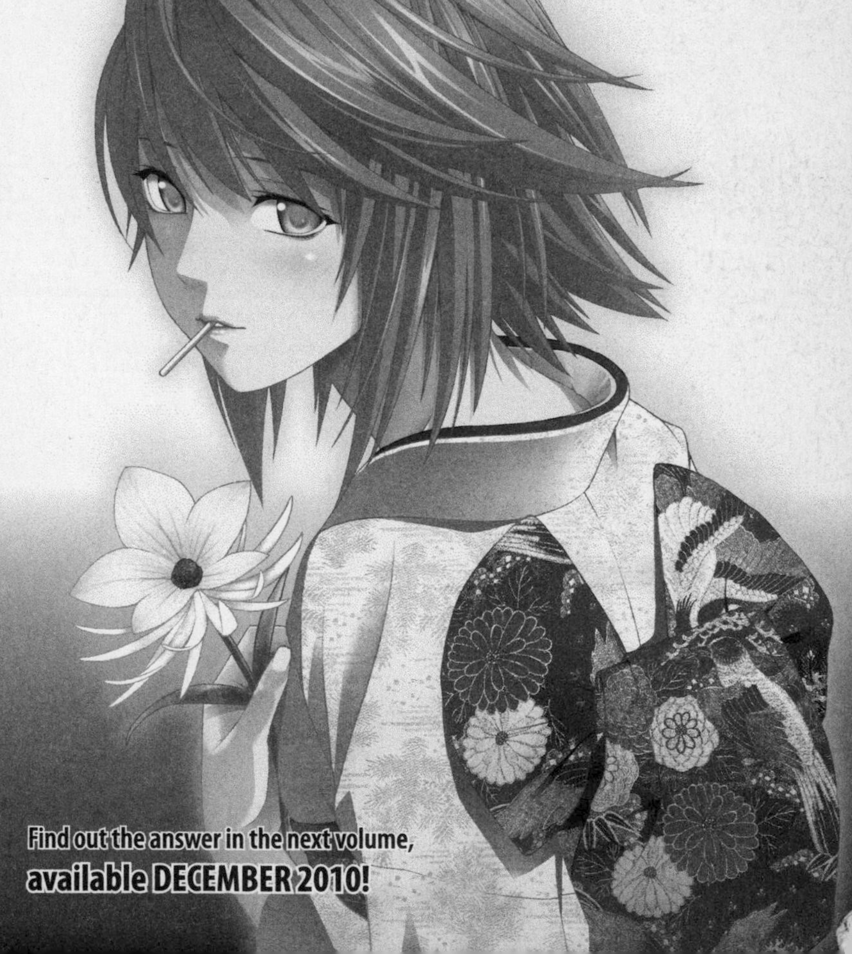

Find out the answer in the next volume,

available DECEMBER 2010!

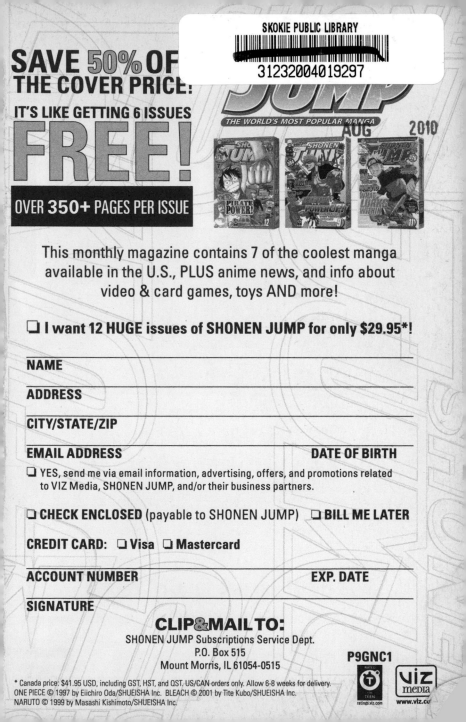